White Lines (Vertical)

Marcelle Freiman was born and grew up in South Africa. Her family originated in Lithuania and Latvia, immigrating to South Africa in the 1930s. Growing up in South Africa during the years of apartheid, she left the country of her birth in 1977, settling in Sydney in 1981. She has two grown sons who live in Hong Kong and London. Her poetry writing coincided with her immigration; as if displacement coupled with memory created an impulse for words and voice. Since 1986 she has published poetry in literary magazines in Australia and overseas, and her poems have been read on radio and in performance. Her first book of poems *Monkey's Wedding* (1995) was highly commended for the Mary Gilmore Prize. The visual arts inspire her writing, particularly her work with the Sydney poetry group DiVerse who write and perform in response to art works in Australian art galleries.

She completed her doctorate on the writer J. M. Coetzee in 1994 and is currently Senior Lecturer in creative writing and literature in the Department of English, Macquarie University. Her scholarly publications include essays on creativity and writing in the journal *TEXT*, and essays on poetry, literature and migration.

Also by Marcelle Freiman

Monkey's Wedding (Island Press Co-operative Ltd 1995)

WHITE LINES (VERTICAL)

Marcelle Freiman

Published by Hybrid Publishers

Melbourne Victoria Australia

© Marcelle Freiman

First published 2010

National Library of Australia Cataloguing-in-Publication data:

Author: Freiman, Marcelle.

Title: White lines (vertical) / Marcelle Freiman.

ISBN: 9781876462970 (pbk.)

Dewey Number: A821.3

Cover design by Gittus Graphics
Typeset in 10.5/15 pt Adobe Garamond Pro

The painting reproduced on the front cover is by
Tony Tuckson: *White lines (vertical) on ultramarine* (1970–73)
diptych: synthetic polymer paint on hardboard, 213.5 x 244.6 cm
board overall
Gift of Annette Dupree 1976
Collection: Art Gallery of New South Wales
© Reproduced with permission

Contents

II

III

IV

Acknowledgments

Poems in this collection have been published, some in slightly different form, in the following publications: *Blast, Blue Dog, Five Bells, Kunapipi, Light on Don Bank: Fifteen Years of Live Poets* (S. Hicks and D. Gardner eds), *Mascara, Matrix, Poetry Without Borders* (Michelle Cahill ed.), *Prismatics: Poets Union Anthology 2008* (John L. Sheppard ed.), *Quadrant, Scarp, Southerly, Sunlines* (A. Fairbairn ed.), *The Honey Fills the Cone: Newcastle Poetry Prize Anthology 2006, Westerly, Wet Ink.*

Gate

That moment on a day
like any other day, or hour,
when walking the uneven path,
watching for stones, tree roots,
things that trip you up
no matter how you'd rather
avoid the night –
you come – face to the glass,
nose to the stone, you arrive
that minute, that second
like a bird's wing up against
the grain, the wood, the tree,
the board, the gate,
the bend in the road
that stops your tracks, stops you –
and you break in two, in three,
looking all the while straight ahead
for that forceful shining thing
you know you've lost

I

A German Cubism

Lyonel Feininger (1871-1956)

Whose God was shining through your surfaces?
The cathedral opens like a window
bright as the face of Moses –
you turned the stone of steeple into glass
as if your eye had broken open.

Blue sky-tinted panes ascend
that belief might loosen its face,
on your sliding pages are letters of gold,
their awe carved upon the night of Sinai –
though the tablets were shattered in fury
they hang upon the air
written
like souls released from ovens.

In the eye before the storm, the cathedral
swings from its darkness,
turns over in its bed like a lantern.
Your art makes a glass façade
in which we see our million broken faces:
you have cut through stone
space slides over surfaces of time
the glass has moth-wings of malachite.

Open Lace-work

Russia 1992

A row of white milestones –
silver birch forests strike past the train,
I remember the lift and tug
of a language soft as wrapped chords
– and hands of women
their fingers drawing threads in a cloth
of open-work: spaces like halts
and absences on a journey,
a lace of silver-white stitches
laid on my grandmother's table.

We drink black tea from glasses
in silver holders etched with leaves,
hold conserved strawberries
on our tongues – through which
acrid tea passes our lips:
I see my grandfather long ago,
a long-handled spoon in his glass
lifting to his mouth
the whole-grape jam my grandmother made
to sweeten his tea.

Though such things
were refused in our house of marble and stone,
a new language and a family scattered

like branches across a forest floor –
they are words from the dark years
etched like cut-glass
on our skin

in rooms warm with coal,
the steam of a samovar
draws me back
on threads of smoke.

The Hairdresser c. 1950

For my grandmother Leah

The fanlight window of the barber shop
webs a fretwork
of black lead and bubbled glass,
sun-ray pattern muffles the street outside.
In the yellow light
grandmother stands behind a woman
whose frizzed red hair she perms,
looking up, sees herself framed –
       bottles of hair oil, tonics, dyes,
white washbasins and barbers' chairs,
their leather worn to a shine
       silver bases like upturned goblets –

she spins her web of coloured hair,
frail threads tie her to the past
held by filaments
soft as the chrysanthemums
printed flamingo pink on her pale green gown
of silk,
       its touch on her skin
like the soft-weave cocoons
of fat silkworms fed on
beetroot leaves from the garden
before they turn to pale feathered moths –

her hands make a glass-house, rooms
of stitched flowers, polished wood,
over and over she recreates
        young faces in the mirror,
their eyes a sepia gloss
like her father, her brothers,
caught in grainy photographs
their corners pinned
on black paper pages
in the album on the high shelf.

In her rooms
sleek cushions, tassels, satin sofas
smooth to the touch
of fingers roughened and stained
with harsh soap –
now with hair-dye.

Drawing

You know the raw play
of objects – how the force
pulls at an embryo
preys on the hovering seed.
It's the tiny thing
ready to soak up life –
the just-hatched bird
feathers still wet, bones soft
holding the match-flame in its hand
despite the tooth-faced
ready to devour,
grinning, insatiable.

Furnace

The cupola furnace
the heating furnace
the iron melting furnace
the furnace for hands to tie iron
into knots, into chains
the furnace for the boiler
the red heat, white heat
the conflagration, the fire
that burned the priests
who looked upon their god,
the men who reached too far
the men who glutted themselves
the men who ordered the world
the ones who harnessed fire
the lists of names, the numbers, the records
the factories, the chimneys, the ashes
the smoke from the ovens
the white heat of the furnace
the blackening heat of shrapnel
the noise of steam hammers
the silence after burning.

Normal

'… a generation that has witnessed nothing but war'
— Stephen Dupont

He is seated against a wall
shaft of sunlight through the window,
knee bent, sole clasped in his hand,
his body at rest with tea and sweet sugar,
as if the day – normal as a potted plant
placed in the window's light
has his life stitched to a tapestry of gestures –
as if each day would like to amble
like red and gold knots of wool on a loom,
tufting the years in the old patterns,
and to pray five times from sunrise to sunset
means this day will step
exactly as its forebears –
but there's just one minute
before the light-beam shift,
before darkness will shadow the room,
the tea grow cold in its copper,
his prayers be answered meagerly – with guns,
his face is already turned, not to be blinded.

War

i. Child

What will hold her, fingers
clinging to the wire,
small singlet smudged
with ash?
She'll breathe the smells
of burnt rubber and cane
where palm-trees of her play-time
had stood – in flames –
and never forget
how seeking shelter
he pushed her
and the empty cart
along the road.

ii. Dili

as if a human hurricane came through,
as if heartbeat and breath were less than
nothing, less than a blackened tree,
bent-metal pieces
debris pushed into ditches,
as if there would be nothing
to answer – as if the air
could be silenced
the eyes of trees closed –

as if all this were done
with no breath of expiation

iii. Suai

the church altar opens its mouth
to the sky
bullet-pocked and bloodied walls,
the screams of massacre
written in the air
and no-one to answer

The Camp

Impossible now
to say nothing – it's still
the held-down body
the fences and dogs

the madness that makes
of his life's succour
a dream behind a window –
this thing we know
how to do so well:
imprison what we fear.

We have learned nothing.

He cries on the pallet,
the dogs are not a dream
the archway
is remembering.

Lightening

So this is what it comes to –
excised from our vision
of what we believed
beyond the clean-cut mathematical
stone-carved monument,
we built columned allegories
granite upon the earth
to memorialize the dead –

the edifice is nothing more than
façade that covers
our brittle memories.

She comes
through the visaged world,
cut from sandstone, kissed by wind and sun
sensuous lick of the old man's tongue –
friable pink pillar, lightening, she loves
the way weather's moulding her skin –

the mountain is not static
this is not Lot's wife
the country is unstable as water.

Beyond

I remember once how the clouds
crossing the moon at night,
swift and indigo and silver
were a sign that after my fragile days
nights like this would breathe –

each momentary heartbeat
must know the vulnerable word
for itself – each toughening
leaf of eucalyptus
stays to write a life.

Masha

Preamble

'the diasporic imagination is steeped
in continuous ambivalence'

Walking round the edges of my self
I draw lines of time and terrain,
each day is clear blue autumn
each hour and minute fragments and spins,
my feet on the ground,
my heart in days and nights of other places –

I had rolled off the edge of South Africa –
in England northern light was thin as a weak light-bulb
while I searched London phone-lists
for my mother's cousin Max –
journalist, Marxist, writer,
his letters from London had come like birds
into my postbox in that yellow-grass country,
my girlhood had craved him,
but now the city swallowed
his face, time emptied of him,
left white stones along the road –

[18]

four years later landed in Sydney,
carved free of South African, I thought,
but the rift of it was a river-bed pared to bone,
made me cold, dust-specks in my eyes in spite of this sun
I was living all faceted and backwards –
until one day memories of my grandmother's voice
began to echo in the words of my mouth,
in every Hebrew letter on the page
each ancestral story of doubt and loss
kissed its lips to my forgetting –
like Jonah coughed out of the whale
taught me how to live this life.

What shoes do I wear?
no longer backward, but time won't let go,
this journey embraces and makes strange –
I look for signs of meaning,
at every rut and turn in the road
memories demand my words.

Hearts and clubs

'O brave new world,
That has such people in't!'

Like Alice I fall into lights,
hearts and spades, a gamble
of games, Lightning Strike, roulette
(sans croupier the game winks its lights,
flashes its bling) – I miss the satiny arms

of a skilled woman in sequin gown, dealing
diamonds and clubs, the click of chips
smooth turn of wheel, my lucky thirty-six –
a poker machine brings Queen of the Nile,
did Cleopatra play Roulette with the asp?
last win one seventy eight dollars fifty four,
another says Pompei in brash Vegas lettering,
resurrects the pleasure-city poster-style,
unexplained a duck flies past repeatedly,
something like Lightning Strike, Lucky
chance, take it. Everyone wants to win –
the man in jacket and yellow tie patterned
with a mosaic of yellow diamonds, dressed for Sunday,
a woman leans far back on her stool, tipped to fall –
and upstairs in the Gold Star Room banner
the twelve tribes, their gateway flanked with trophies
say it's all about men's names and Football Heaven –
I'm spinning in the empty room
without cleats my boots won't hold,
like Alice splashing through her pool of tears
I slide through the door, and out

Cumin

A lunch of falafel, cumin, chilli,
hummus and Hebrew voices – and I'm back
in a country of trees loaded with pomelos,
pink-mouthed prickly pears, orange-blossom,
yellow geckoes splay-legged on a white wall,
smell of cyprus, pine, tamarisk,
a white sand road,

time layers moments like stones in a wall –
I remember how young he was, the boy
who photographed goats by an olive tree,
carved the middles from baby marrows
stuffed with rice, cumin, lemon, tahini,
who said, while drawing the shape of walls
on a Jerusalem rooftop 'when the hands are busy
the mind is free'

Museum

a thread of cotton
enough to imagine
imagine a coat
a coat against the cold
the frozen forest floor
ground without sun
dark as hard peat
hard eyes, hard faces
thread of cotton caught
tangled in her hair
her hair the life of
no dust can dull
no peat-black face
no lead nor mud
can quell, her hair tied back
her brow clear milk
the red cotton thread
caught in the frozen

Poland

Hebrew letters adorn suffering Christ
Kadosh, kadosh – intended to punish
the goldsmith, they shine bright against the sky.

We have come to learn Ghetto history,
around us the room is light
with paintings of trees of life.

In the Ghetto no tree allowed to grow
no place of pleasure remained:
still they sang, their lives raw,

they wrote stories in pencil,
drew pictures on paper, sealed pages in milk urns,
hoped for resurrection of readers.

No memorial can equal their words:
when figures on monuments are muscled in stone
so still they void memory of bone and hunger – then how to tell

of the woman who rescued a child,
after the war sought advice to baptize
from the priest who said 'tell her
she is Jewish, find a Jewish family
to care for her'

– such stories are not told
in the language of suffering:
these stories light windows of gold and blue glass.

Epilogue

My grandmother received a telegram,
news of her mother sister cousins perished in Simna,
all that waiting, not knowing – then silence,
it made her stomach burn, made her never
let anything be lost again.
I trail this history along with the light
of my fortunate travels. Through her loss
she gave me everything

and I ask – is my remembering
mapped in buildings
or when I walk under trees, wondering
what will become of the mallards
when ponds in Centennial Park go dry –
and what will we become
when the stranger is turned from the door?
– or is it found in the clean bark of a snow-gum
cool to touch, branches crossed
against the sky as if to say 'here
rest your hand, be held'.

Oasis

If my bedding was carried
in a bag of cloth, rich with patterns
woven red, orange and black
over dunes on the slow-bellied rhythm
of a camel's back
sailing beneath stars in the cool nights
resting in the burning days
by an oasis fringed with palms
where coffee is shared, figs and dates
to sweeten the midday silence
broken only by camel bells
the necessary word,
the prayer at sunset –
then my dreams
would thread intricate colours
my days be carpets of peace.

II

The Enamel Plate

For my grandmother Chana

It was light in the kitchen, smooth enamel plates
on a table, house in the veld, a Dutch interior
sunlit with square windows, corners
of a piano and picture frames.
Why this memory over and over?
I could pivot on a thread between this house

and my childhood home in a city of gold:
dark-skinned nannies with their warm backs
could disappear in the night – I remember waking
one morning in the south-facing house – shadowed rooms,
frosted-glass doors, the green unyielding sofa,
I ran to the kitchen, barefoot, expecting
her at the kitchen-sink, glass of milk ready –
but the kitchen light was off in the morning cold
'Sarah (or Vyna) has gone'.

No goodbye –
as if her plump presence, her shoulder,
could be replaced like the cat
when it thumped under the wheels of a car:
I lay on the cold floor, its hardness on my back

then the car-ride to the dusty town,
where this sunlit house like a Dutch interior

held me still as a lodestone – hands
could be trusted to stay: the clatter of pans
on the coal stove before dawn, the bright
enamel plate on the table, blue rimmed,
a call to prayer: my grandmother,
her arms held wide over the stove
like wings.

In Our House

She sang and swayed her hips
polishing the parquet,
a tongue-click in her voice like a bell,
and I crouched at her warm hip,
our knees on the gritty floor,
the piney wax-polish in its tin

> *she was my nanny, carried me on her back, my face against her*
> *cotton dress, so clean and washed I breathed the smell of the sun*
> *and a hot iron on fabric*

afternoons we'd sit on the concrete path
beside the house in the sun,
she'd push her white *doek*
to the back of her head, and I was shy
to see her naked ears, her hair soft combed wool,
her lunch on the cream plate,
brown bread, peanut-butter
tea in the blue mug:
afternoon was her tired time
she'd lean her back against the wall

> *she bathed and dressed me, ironed shirts and pants and*
> *underpants, peeled carrots and potatoes, sliced paw-paws and*
> *oranges, dusted venetian blinds, stirred pots of beef and chicken,*
> *folded sheets, swept verandas, dusted bookshelves*

when we crossed the road
she'd hold me –
my life in her hands:
her voice was
in every room.

Masque

The forced gaiety of it,
the mad smiles,
pot-lid masks, nursery school paint,
battered, bent and bow-legged
like children made mad by the lie.

This is a masquerade
of what we were told to expect,
that we'd be happy and safe:

when buttons batter noise,
when grey grimace red tongue
and teeth rust, the sharp thrust,
children blind with fright,
the tear-torn eye –

memories heap upon the pile
laced with lattices of corrosion –
the dust balls under the bed,
leaden hearts, like crushed metal,
ash fallen from a father's cigarette,
a mother torn of sex,
children delivered to it –

the sky was filled with planes
aiming at our picnic.

No *hoffnung* nor *liebe* –
the remains were yellow as a cat's eye
shining through the mud.

Beetles

Down the passage of a house,
Picasso's harlequin on white wall,
kilim rug red-green-blue on wooden floor,
ink drawings on a whitewashed wall,
then outside watching beetles in the grass
beneath the bottle-brush – your hand
on my shoulder was strong,
blue wash and harlequin were like nothing
in this brown land,
but there was sky and grass
and watching beetles –
dung-beetle shiny black carapace,
one on another's back.
        We shivered
not knowing why, your hands grew
larger on my back –
children watching beetles
imprinted on the sand – and I loved
how your skin was warm.

1971

It was time for a new world,
against apartheid, our own war:
it was dagga, rough with twigs, in 'fingers' or 'arms'
bought from the kid in the township,
smoked in its brown paper wrapping, seeds popping
on a South Coast beach, watching an empty bottle
bashing itself in the foam and rocks.

Police paranoia, threw half an arm from the car window
into a starlit night,
Peter going psychotic, getting schizoid,
his body moving on Largactil,
his brilliance falling like Icarus –
then time stopped, threw his watch into the sea,
ten years later in prison for shooting a guard on a train
because, he said, he wore a uniform.

Josiah the night watchman in our building,
'Wise Old Af' in his old greatcoat
sold dagga on the rooftop, shared his pipe,
waiting for the struggle to end, *knobkerrie* in his belt,

and we marched through Joburg streets
against 90 and 180 Days Detention Without Trial Laws,
and prison even for white boys. Trying to forget
about John Vorster Square and the SAP,

searched in Durban for DP, and found it,
eating dope cookies in the car all the way to Cape Town,
having to stop in the karoo afternoon to have sex,
wild thorn-bush and shimmering acacias in the heat,
place of red sunsets and crashing seas,
swimming naked in the freezing Atlantic at night,
sunrise eating smoked fish on the rocks at Hout Bay.

Slow time, staying child-like
when guilt and white privilege could turn you crazy,
and mostly
it was driving you, with each drag, closer and closer to your
      country.

Smokes

First drag at fourteen
wanting to be glossy
like *Seventeen,*
belly armoured,
breasts (the punches)
with rose-nipples,
those boys hating softness.

Tough then, smoking,
black leather jacket,
studs in a wrist-band,
unfiltered Lucky's,
Gitanes or Camels,
no Gold Band filter
or menthol cool –

just tobacco bits
right on your tongue,
this was how to be strong,
wipe them out,
take a man's drag,
show them.

Oak

The lesson card from England
pointed to the oak as 'native tree'
and singing *O Danny Boy* and *My Bonnie*,
our childish voices lifting
to green hills and valleys,
we learned how we'd never be at home
in the veld and dusty kikuyu grass
outside the classroom windows –
birth-written by our whiteness
either to rule or leave.

England called us: better there
the ordered world, safe –
but we'd pine like animals
for the smell of African sand
strong as flint,
strong in our veins.

The summer we travelled to Stonehenge
my hands turned to artefacts
I was seeking my history
in the broken circle of stones,
as if my language would assure
and the moon of De La Mare
would shed its silver, cool as mercury:

but the emigrant
had lost her words –
white puppet on a stalk
turned her face again to find the sun
where the earth is red stubble,
on a blue Pacific coast
with pink hibiscus.

I count the years since leaving the yellow veld:
in the fifth the puppet petals dropped,
the eighth I sent a tapestry,
patterns of words on canvas
threaded with the brown and gold
of sand and memories:
the year our Sydney garden
was shaded by an old oak tree
I rubbed my back against her crusty bark
like an antelope itching with dust.

Fences

Johannesburg

I. Number 27

Campbell Street, Waverley

I return to a street of my childhood, now gated –
back then the house was unfenced, the tarmac road
a jacaranda walk to the bus-stop,
smell of tree resin, sticky beetles,
in 1960 my wings beginning to stretch.

       How to say
       that this distant place was home,
       that the heart, half-empty, was everything?

Look down the throat
of the blue crane's open beak,
crack the memory of the speckled shell
to yoke a blue sky morning
to these spiked fences, razor-wired, electric:

       then, we were blind with dust and sun – white grubs
       bedded in suburban lawns,
       in tree-bark, wriggling for life
       in our cardigans and red dungarees.

Now wires hum above high fences,
lock the white pupas in:
how will they emerge, these children?

Today the street is hard to breathe in
though grey doves croon in winter stillness,
a gardener digs by the gate, waves a smile,
palm trees rustle on a dry wind:

        and I remember the late-night cries,
        the agony of a man with no feeling in his legs,
        blood pooled, seeped into the gravel,
        bicycle-spoke in his spine –
        the iron of his blood.

        Is memory the illusion
        that we were rooted here
        with the giant bluegums
        growing on the boundary?

We are forgotten traces,
the road is clean,
razor wire glints high in the sun:

who remembers the butterfly?
it hovered once
for a full minute above a garden bed
of purple columbines.

II. Barking Dogs

Seventh Avenue, Highlands North

At 49 dogs are barking:
the curved veranda, red-cement *stoep*,
the window bars, unchanged

since 1954 – I remember
dogs barked here then
in the yard, by the low gate,
watchdogs, their melting eyes turned vicious
wild at a passer-by on his bicycle.

Was the air more friendly
than this high-walled fortress
where a family now lives
angry in South Africa?

More fear permeates the street
than dust in sunlight –
in this city of aloes,
its half-lived pretence,
the lie-cheating truth
of home –
the story has come undone:
you can feel its sound, hear it
as you always did
in the barking of dogs.

III. Winter Morning

The distant sound of mini-bus taxis skidding, vying for fares,
        the fight
to commute on Modderfontein Road,
traffic hum, sirens, voices – I am separate from the hardness,
still blessed with privilege, who questions it? I'm greeted with love –
and the history of the old oppression is vivid,
raw in roofless frost of a Highveld morning,
the struggle to work and live despite AIDS and TB, despite
        the lost children:
the women are bright eyed with death.

Birds greet in yellow morning frost,
women's voices fill the day as they walk to their work,
there's garbage in street gutters –
yesterday a white man screamed 'bloody fucking bitch' as I turned
        a corner:
bitterness lives in every stone:
beneath words of greed and placation there's a great wound here,
but rich voices sing hymns, love Madiba, resolve *ubuntu* –
        all is one –

and there's the smoking smell of morning, water running over
        pelindaba rocks
in the Jukskei River at the edge of this gated-village,
blond stone warms in slow sunshine, wild geese preen and *kwaak*
        on the rocks,
shake speckled wings, flash of green and white, calling as they lift
        their bodies,

graceful crosses against the sky, their heads lit crowns of sun.
The river runs past Alexandria township, past our fences,
plastic bags and bottles litter the banks, the water foams,
I watch through three layers of wire, the third, most recent,
    electric:
a man washes his face and rib-cage in the river, crouched on a
    sand-coloured rock,
a grey and brown *mossie* hops under the lowest wire rung,
another perched on the fence-top ignores the razor barbs,
a yellow weaverbird hangs upside down from the farthest end of
    the thinnest branch
of a wild seringa tree, safe from predators,
its black-masked head darts and weaves,
    builds a bottle-shaped nest,
intricate beak-woven fabric of grasses.

If the death-wish of apartheid's crime has harmed
every rock and fire-scorched tussock of veld
with its smell of rusted cans and burnt rubber –
it fights in the marrow of the children on their way to school
who want to stretch out each minute of book-learning –
and life is pulsing, I can taste it in the smoke of morning,
in the patience of the weaver,
in the strong arms of the women, their loud voices.

III

The Factory

I remember him in his study, a photograph
of Albert Schweitzer at his shoulder
or sitting on the verandah at the end of the day
sweet caramel smoke of his pipe,
stars of an African night
tears of dew caught in the wool
of his cardigan, the wool of his hair, like pearls –

in my father's factory
the other side of the city
workers shovelled coal in the heat,
their shouts firing the boiler for the cooling tower,
the steel pylons and concrete wide against the sky:
a plant to manufacture food –
great steel vats fermenting nutrients
for *Puza Mandla*, sour drink made from maize –
in warehouse stores its white dust peppered floors
of corridors between piles of sacks, danced
in the sun shafting through the windows –
and *Protone*, a soup of soya, mixed with water
could feed a starving child
for a penny each day.

How many children stayed bright eyed, their skin firm
against *kwashiorkor* in Rwanda, the Congo, Transkei?
did the boy later become the soldier
or remain white-shirted schoolboy, then teacher

in a village near a river? was the girl who held
the tin cup of soup in her hands
belly filled with proteins
later a mother killed, her baby still tied
in a blanket on her back, crying by a gravel road?
or does she teach her daughters
to pound maize in a wooden vat,
sit waiting at sunset for the children to return
along the dust road,
their footprints in the red sand?
and what of the prisoners in their island jail
drinking *Puza Mandla,* who awaited apartheid's end
waiting for their freedom?

How to act
beyond the borders of apartheid?
my father dreamed of life
while hunger was everywhere
just one man, he willed to subdue it –
the factory pumps, the rotating cogs,
the cooling tower's mouth to the sky,
echoed his heart-beats
thundered against the horizon –
filled the stomachs of children
and repaired the brightness
to their hungry eyes.

Mercy

Johannesburg, 1988

I watch from the doorway of our house –
Mercy, the nurse, holds my father's hand
leads him slowly to the car,
white headed, stoop-shouldered,
he accepts her strong dry hand.

Mercy tells me of strikes in Soweto –
people told to withhold their rent,
but with no office to approach
when evicted, their boxes,
pots, pans, blankets and clothes scattered
around them on the road.
Government leaflets in their turn say
Do not support the boycott –
yet compliance would risk scorched rubber, a burned house
roofless, her daughters and their children
under a cold burning sky.

Mercy goes to church on Sundays,
prays from a full heart. She walks
through the township dawn,
her wide body a warning
to *tsotsis*.
Each night
she comes from Soweto

to the white suburbs
to care for my father.

When he died she walked
into our house with its candles,
her hips arthritic, bent with stroke, still massive:
round the family table
she held our hands, opened her Bible
closed her eyes, and sang,
her voice like a bell –
you could feel God at her shoulder,
waiting over the horizon.

IV

Spiny Molluscs, Sète

The low hills along the road were sandy
pines bent to the wind, olive-trees dry on stony ground,
the day white-hazed with ozone and seaweed,
our car tracked the bitumen with chalk dust:
we were a blink in time:
Europe was claiming us with its dream
and we ignored how the surface of the water was unnaturally dull
in spite of the light.

The harbour town was quiet, afternoon sun
brownish-yellow as we drove to the quay,
seagulls wheeled overhead, nets were strung up and ringed
with salt-crusted corks, and fishermen unknotting and mending
smoked their pipes and dismissed us with their eyes.
In market stands green mussels and snail shells
moved in glistening heaps, line-fish lay bright-eyed on slabs,
a woman sharpened her knife on the cobble-stones
strewn with fish-scales, pin-bones and fish-guts.

That night we ate plates of raw molluscs
green-shelled, like oysters but gritty with sand,
and a cold slime of spiky sea-urchins in ink –
a second bottle of wine – we were talking
across splinters of shells on the table
(I do not remember what we said):

a day in 1975 – boat hulls creaking by the quay
cry of gulls with darkness falling –
and I watched the bravado of your teeth
cracking crustacean shells, sucking chicken bones,
draining your Chianti, our future still to come –
were we happy? – we were like corks bobbing on water,
smoked Gitanes, spat tobacco bits, got drunk:
easy to disregard the oil and tar
clinging to the soles of our shoes.

Burning Branches

He's burning branches down the back
black smoke and ash-sparks fly into the sun,
sweat streaks his skin, his jeans soaked,
he's opening space, clearing a garden,
eucalyptus crackles orange, pungent,
my eyes smart smoke and grit,
he breaks his way into a new life.

I watch from the back steps,
keep the hose ready,
look out for the children –
with a stick he drags from the fire
a horseshoe – left in a pile of rubbish
crusted russet with age, red-hot
it brands the lawn –
later, I think, I will hang it over the door
for luck.

That night we burn the heavier logs,
old wood, pieces of kitchen chairs,
paint bubbles and spits in the hearth
scorched glow tints our faces amber,
the wooden house creaks,
outside it smells of sap and embers
but clear now, and cold,

stars through uncurtained windows,
no moon – a train cries
in the distance, shunts in the night.

Ginger Plants

Down in the bush-garden gully
looking for ginger flowers –
red orange, winged with yellow, like birds,
the flowers struggle and droop in the heat,
sticky stamens are red wine,
or old blood, dark as prunus in suburban gardens,
sticks and sharp twigs scratch my arms,
ginger stems straggle, edged with straw hairs,
a green wall of bamboo in a gully, craving moisture,
humming with dryness, sick with rotting leaves –
undergrowth shifts at my feet,
at each cut of the hard green flesh
sap runs over my hands
like glue, pinning me to that rift,
to the severed dark green ginger stems,
their leaves folded, paper wings in the heat,
each slice of the knife
comes closer to my skin.

Morphinée

When a dull ache
fingered my belly
turned walnut hard
until a fist of steel
knife-blade in the back
so piercing
nothing was real
but white-heat –

then sting in my hip
kiss of needle
in tender nurse fingers
light as a fly's touch
gauze wing release –
it was love
as the pethidine spread
through my body
like a blessing.

This Country

For Fred Williams

When I landed this place
felt hard-stippled, I could not bear
its crackling harshness –
my fingernail on tough grey leaf
came away oil tinged with memory:
dry-twig bark-stripped ground
hard as berries on bare feet
remnant of my homeland.

I'd returned to the hemisphere of my birth
but the planet was different, *unheimlich*,
could not see my way
to the resurrection I craved,
the thirst for a new starting –

then paintings on a gallery wall
showed ochre and sage on desert gravel
grey as cold clay –
yes, I'd fingered blood-rimmed leaves
in days of forgetting, blood-prints on earth,
on red sand, had forgotten – and now the art
cut loose my clouded vision,
black brush marks, charred wood,
as if it knew my memory, saying

here death lives in every seed,
the land endures everything,
the poetry was always there
it takes a new eye to see.

Slipping on Red Shoes

Playing to your tune
           you had me – we were
characters in a novel –
changing places –
           my blue-tongued land
           a stage for
           your scenario –

my feet slipping
red shoes dancing
on the thin skin of
what I believed
was real –
a road movie with black leather,
red enamel jewels on my toes

in rough pubs on country roads
you strutted
           and I played
your red-painted moll,
my high-heels clicking on the pages.

We'd end the day slumming
in a seedy motel at the edge of a lake
and it seemed you would
pull me from my rooted world
           to the pages of a glossy centrefold –

while all I could feel was
you – loving me
beside a dirt-road
on a steamy morning,
the sound of birds and rain,
> my vision filling
> with a blush of red
> as if my eyes were bleeding.

In Paddington

One afternoon we loved
in the narrow bedroom
of a pitch-roofed house

in Paddington gothic
the courtyard was steamy
February was in lust

the afternoon we loved
painted eaves were mouldy
the bedroom seemed vast

our bodies were sliding
in Sydney summer heat
cicadas were piercing

the leaves were black mould
I called out your name
the room became narrow

the eaves were creaking
the afternoon ending:
its imprint stays in my mind.

Scene in Limbo

Other painters gave us Paris:
the view from a balcony, the wrought iron
and slate-tile roofs leaning majestically,
classic lines of shutters, the forking streets
narrow with gutters and trees in spring –
but how you've shifted the ground – it tilts
and the figures slide, cars and bicycles suspend
in the haze of your playful vision,
the walls soften and smudge, the heraldic eagle
is simply an eagle sitting – walkers topple down
towards the paving-stone surface of my eye
and the balcony leans into my intimate gaze:
the red sign 'no entry' halts everything
and the arms and legs of buildings still want
to fly outwards, as if to embrace what I'll see.

Road

I like streets that go down – Grace Cossington-Smith 1971

It's a road that ribbons down a hill
and up – a velocity, a force
more than a road –

the sky is wide and bright
and the speed of your eye
grabs the horizon –

wanting elsewhere, beyond –
fast as telegraphed voices in the wire,
fast as the line

of the eucalypt that bends its curve
on the surface of your eye
upwards from the purple gully.

How it fights with the walker, this road,
with the slow horse cart,
its line tense

with trees humming green,
edgy with the speed of sound,
the speed of your eye on the road.

Visionary

For Brett Whiteley

Those voyagers pushed out
in little ships, stars and their faith
in compass, plot and angles
their only surety –

but you lived at the pinnacle
acute with wanting
to breach horizons,
strip layers of ego
until the pupa of your heart beat
in air, dissolved your face, glass eye staring
cold, inner eye seeing
lines stripped bare as a bride,
force-fuse, slime, hair,
music of spheres,
each sexual egg a yolk
of paint, bird feather-shell –
and then the sacred baboon,
its mouth filled with blood –

and you did
the dealer's fat finger –
yellow teeth bilge-battle
wanted so much to kill her hand
as you soared like Icarus

because art was always
the main line –

and your ship still pulses,
brazen eyes open
it ploughs into our surfaces,
scores across our pathways
here, up on the headland.

African Heads after Sidney Nolan

Baboon

He knows his territory
in a veld of rusted rocks
the sky heavy with heat and storm,
thunder holds him rigid
square-backed, listening –

aggressive blue-arsed beacon
wire-furred, male tail raised,
sharp-tooth jawed to bite
for each instinct-riven
hunt or lust that drives him.

Lion

Sunlight fires the grassland,
yellow light is dying,
tawny-pelt camouflaged,
yellow-eyes like hemp,
one-toothed old-boy,
mangey-maned hero
blending with the yellow dusk.

Head of Rimbaud

'i and the wind' –
the sun and the line,
horizon melts to sky
black of burnt tree
necklace of grass
ears of air, head of space
losing my edges i am
ubuntu – all and one –
spirit, seed of grass,
i am

Seeds

I.

In the field of rye and red poppies
the sound of ripening
smaller than ants, silent as air –
seeds surge through another summer
and nothing, not even their bitterness,
will stop the breathing.

II.

We soaked white beans in saucers of cotton,
to soften and wrinkle – they'd split,
show their yellow bean-food,
each new shoot and stem and first pale leaf –
we imagined cells dividing and multiplying,
membranes breaking –
planted the pale shoots in dry soil by the back fence,
the water pooled, then sank around fragile stems,
the bean plants threw spiral tendrils to the wire
holding tight, their white pea-flowers
delicate as skin.

III.

Melon seeds drying on the window sill
and pumpkin pips in the sun –
we placed them at the bottom of the garden
near the compost heap – and all through summer

watched those warm white pumpkins swell
under their sheltering umbrella leaves,
heavy stomachs against the earth,
their insides becoming more gold-orange
each day – while the cool white melons ripened
sugar-green flesh, too numerous to harvest,
and by autumn the late seed-pods bent their necks
down towards the compost earth.

Yes

Sometimes we become so tired
in our heavy walk
tread on brittle insects
with our difficult boots
and small dogs with side-glance eyes
become wary of even our knotted hands –
but yes – clear as a white lit river
it comes through our day, this curving seam
from who knows where –
and bright through bladed grass,
and the angles of our buildings,
on the streets we walk with our thick shoes –
yes, still it comes.

Visitation

The hot early morning demands
I release
the green-gold-black butterfly
beating its thorax, tearing its wings
on the glass inside my window –
only I can end this – and it flies upwards
into sunshine for its one-day of life
leaving dark chewed-foliage drops
of its terrified waste
on the white-painted frame:

marks of dried charcoal stain
shear across the day –
so that something wing-driven
might open its shoulders
to clamor and deafen the morning.

The days don't hear
what is dying
if I were to let my love
stiffen as my body
does: it does not go
peacefully
just because a few words
colored green-gold-black
will be washed away
by the rain.

Intuitively

To such blue as heavens,
where stars cut through
and satellites cross the sky,
we send out messages
in hours, in air –

this is not a dialogue:
intuitive the word
speaks to brush-stroke,
white to blue to brown –

everything depends upon
the slash diagonal, the crossing,
branching where two parts join –
a mighty thrust
white heat momentum
ultramarine of infinite,
more than cool, deeper than time,
it flies even as it covers the tracks
it made on the ground.

Glossary

doek – headscarf

DP – *Durban Poison*, marijuana

John Vorster Square – Security Police headquarters in
     Johannesburg.

knobkerrie – short wooden club with a heavy knob on one end

kwashiorkor – disease of malnutrition

kwaak – phonetical, based in Afrikaans, of a particular bird
     sound. Own rendition.

Puza Mandla – powdered drink made from fermented maize

Protone – powdered soup based on soy with added nutrients

tsotsis - township gangsters

ubuntu – post-apartheid idea of connectedness, promoted by Rev.
     Desmond Tutu.

Notes

References and quotations in the poem 'Masha' are from Leopold Shaff quoted in a caption at The Jewish Museum, Sydney; from Ien Ang (1993) 'Migrations of Chineseness', *SPAN*, No 34/35, 1992/1993: 4; from Shakespeare's *The Tempest*, V: i 183; from Paul O'Shea's class on 'Holocaust Pilgrimage: Seeing with the eyes, Listening with the Heart', Shalom Institute, UNSW, May 2006. 'The Factory' refers Nutritional Foods Pty Ltd, the company founded by my father Mair Rosenberg and his partner Mrs Mutzi Grand in Industria, Johannesburg in 1955. The factory, manufacturing nutritionally formulated powdered foods, is still operating under different owners and continues to produce *Protone* and *Puza Mandla*.

I would like to acknowledge many paintings, drawings and photographs, most by Australian artists, for their inspiration in the following poems: 'A German Cubism': Lionel Feininger, Der Ostchor des Domes zu Halle *(1931)*; 'Drawing': Robert Klippel, Drawing P19 *(1949)*; 'War': Stephen Dupont, Dili burns as a man pushes a cart with a small child on board *(1999)*, Rick Amor, Destruction in Dili *and* Atrocity site: church altar, Suai *(1999)*; 'The Camp': Klaus Friedeberger, Camp Dream *(1943)*; 'Lightening': James Gleeson, The Attitude of Lightning towards a Lady-mountain *(1939)*; 'Masque': Colin Lanceley, The Glad Family Picnic *(1961-62)*; 'Beetles': Donald Friend, Boys Watching Beetle *(c. 1960s)*; 'African Heads after Sidney Nolan': Sidney Nolan, Baboon (1963), Lion (1963), Head of Rimbaud (1963), quote 'i and the wind' from Sidney Nolan, Notebook March 16 1952; 'This Country': Fred Williams, You Yangs Landscape *(1963)*; 'Scene in Limbo': Margaret Olley Place

Dauphine, Paris 1951 (ink and watercolour on paper); *'Yes': Kevin Connor,* Figure in a Haymarket Winter Park *(1963); 'Intuitively': Tony Tuckson,* White Lines (vertical) on Ultramarine *(1970-73).*